£7.99

A Pillar Box Red Publication

**Photography © Big Pictures.co.uk**

**ISBN: 978-1-907823-17-6**

**© 2011. Published by Pillar Box Red Publishing Ltd.**

This is an independent publication.

It is completely unofficial and unauthorised and, as such, has no connection with the artist or artists featured, or with any organisation or individual connected in any way whatsoever with the artist or artists featured.

Any quotes within this publication which are attributed to the celebrity, or celebrities, featured have been sourced from other publications, or from the internet, and, as such, are a matter of public record.

They have not been given directly to the author by the celebrity, or celebrities, themselves.

Whilst every effort has been made to ensure the accuracy of information within this publication, the publisher shall have no liability to any person or entity with respect to any inaccuracy, misleading information, loss or damage caused directly or indirectly by the information contained within this book.

The views expressed are solely those of the author and do not reflect the opinions of Pillar Box Red Publishing Ltd. All rights reserved.

# we love you... RIHANNA

## AN UNAUTHORISED 2012 ANNUAL

Written by Sarah Milne

Designed by Nicky Regan

| | |
|---|---|
| 8 | From The Beginning |
| 10 | Then |
| 11 | Now |
| 12 | Wordsearch |
| 14 | All About Ri |
| 16 | Discography |
| 18 | Live On Stage |
| 20 | Collaborations |
| 22 | Other Ventures |
| 26 | Hairstyles |
| 28 | Crossword |
| 30 | Fashion |
| 32 | Famous Friends |
| 36 | Influences |
| 39 | Quiz Time |
| 40 | Match Up! |
| 42 | Give The Girl An Award |
| 44 | Fact Or Fiction |
| 46 | Rihanna Navy |
| 48 | Spot The Difference |
| 50 | Charity Work |
| 52 | Say What... |
| 56 | Rihanna's Favourite Things |
| 58 | A-Z Of Rihanna |
| 60 | Quiz Answers |

# FROM THE BEGINNING

**RIHANNA HAS COME A LONG WAY SINCE SHE WAS DISCOVERED BY CHANCE IN 2003, AND HAS PACKED IN LOTS OF SUCCESS. HERE'S A QUICK RUN DOWN OF HER EARLY PROGRESS...**

Born on February 20, 1988, in Saint Michael, Barbados, Robyn Rihanna Fenty's parents, Monica and Ronald were from Guyana and Barbados respectively – it's said that her dad has some Irish ancestry too. The couple have two more children, Rihanna's younger brothers Rorrey and Rajad. The singer remains very close to her mother and brothers, but has had a difficult relationship with her father – her parents split when she was just 14.

While at school Rihanna was in a musical trio with a couple of her classmates, and in 2003 some friends introduced Rihanna and her band mates to record producer Evan Rogers (who happened to be holidaying in Barbados at the time). The group were allowed to audition for Rogers, who admits that he was blown away by RiRi as soon as he saw her, saying: "the minute Rihanna walked into the room, it was like the other two girls didn't exist." Rihanna sang a cover of Destiny's Child's cover of Emotion, and Rogers knew he had a star in the making

In the year that followed, Rihanna and mum Monica flew back and forth from Barbados to Rogers' house in Connecticut, USA, and when the singer turned 16 in 2004 she moved in with Rogers and his wife.

In collaboration with Carl Sturken and Rogers, Rihanna recorded a four-track demo, which included what would become her first hit, Pon de Replay. The demo landed in Def Jam's offices, and listened to by Jay-Z (president of Def Jam at the time), who quickly signed her.

Pon de Replay was released in 2005, became a global hit, reaching the top ten in the charts of 10 different countries. Not bad for a first attempt. This girl had only one place to go, and that was to the top!

# WORDSEARCH

| | | | | | | | | | | | |
|---|---|---|---|---|---|---|---|---|---|---|---|
| L | U | F | H | T | I | A | F | N | U | R | V | K |
| N | T | T | V | W | L | M | R | F | T | R | T | R |
| D | U | O | L | T | A | Q | R | Y | E | P | P | Q |
| T | X | K | M | J | B | B | N | B | N | Y | K | Y |
| Y | B | D | F | A | Y | G | L | G | N | L | E | L |
| Z | R | E | V | M | D | F | V | L | X | S | V | N |
| P | D | X | M | N | L | O | J | L | F | O | E | T |
| V | X | A | G | E | B | F | N | N | H | D | I | A |
| G | R | D | U | N | G | Y | K | N | R | A | L | T |
| G | W | R | T | H | V | T | V | M | A | B | E | T |
| U | M | B | R | E | L | L | A | A | B | R | B | O |
| P | Y | V | D | G | M | H | B | J | N | A | N | O |
| L | B | O | B | M | A | R | L | E | Y | B | M | B |

*Can you find all 11 words linked to Rihanna? Words can be vertical, horizontal, diagonal or backwards.*

Answers on page 60.

BARBADOS
BELIEVE
BOBMARLEY
DEFJAM
GRAMMY
LOUD
MADONNA
NAVY
REBLFLEUR
TATTOO
UMBRELLA

# ALL ABOUT RI

**Name:** Rihanna.

**Born:** February 20, 1988.

**Place of birth:** Saint Michael, Barbados,

**Nationality:** Bajan/Guyanese.

**Hair:** Changeable – most likely red at the moment.

**Eyes:** Brown/Hazel.

**Height:** 5'9".

**Starsign:** Rihanna was born on the cusp, so her sign can change from year to year. Some years it's Aquarius, others it's Pisces.

**Family:** Two younger brothers.

**Pets:** DJ, an Apricot Toy Poodle

**Record label:** Def Jam Records.

**Debut Single:** Pon de Replay.

**First UK number 1:** Umbrella (also topped the iTunes download charts in 17 countries).

Ri-Ri was an army cadet while at school – she probably managed to look great, even in the uniform!

Rihanna was just 16 when she moved from Barbados to the US and firstly lived with record producer Evan Rogers and his wife in Connecticut.

Rihanna loves tattoos – her thirteenth inking reads *"Never a failure, always a lesson"* and is written backwards so she can read it in the mirror.

Our girl loves to help others – Rihanna set up the Believe Foundation in 2006, to help terminally ill children.

Her heritage is exotic – mother is from Guyana, South America, and she's rumoured to have some Irish blood too.

Rihanna loves fashion, and in April 2011 appeared on the cover of US Vogue, a great honour.

# DISCOGRAPHY

To date, Rihanna has released 8 albums (including 3 compilations), 34 singles and 25 music videos. Not bad for someone who just started in 2005!

## 2005

**SINGLES**

Pon de Replay (debut single went Platinum in Australia and US)

If It's Lovin' That You Want

**ALBUM**

Music of the Sun

## 2006

**SINGLES**

SOS (Platinum in US)

Unfaithful (Platinum in US)

We Ride

Break It Off

**ALBUM**

A Girl Like Me (2 x Platinum in Canada and Ireland)

## 2007

**SINGLES**

Umbrella (3 x Platinum in US)

Shut Up And Drive (Platinum in US)

Don't Stop the Music (3 x Platinum in US)

Hate That I Love You (Platinum in US)

**ALBUM**

Good Girl Gone Bad (5 x Platinum in UK and Canada)

## 2008

**SINGLES**

Take a Bow (2 x Platinum in US)

Disturbia (4 x Platinum in US)

Rehab

## 2009

**SINGLES**

Russian Roulette

Hard (Platinum in US)

**ALBUMS**

Rated R (2 x Platinum in UK)

Good Girl Gone Bad, the Remixes

3 CD Collector's Set

## 2010

**SINGLES**

Rude Boy (2 x Platinum in US)

Rockstar 101

Te Amo

Only Girl (in the world) (4 x Platinum in Australia)

What's My Name (2 x Platinum in US)

Raining Men

**ALBUMS**

Loud (4 x Platinum in UK)

Rated R Remixed

## 2011

**SINGLES**

S&M (4 x Platinum in Australia)

Man Down

California King Bed (Platinum in Australia)

Rihanna doesn't seem to be one of those people who likes to work alone – she loves to collaborate with artists from all different types of music, and sees the benefit in sharing ideas and talent with others. This open approach to working has led her to some great joint projects, and here are a few of our favs...

## AS A FEATURED ARTIST

| | |
|---|---|
| 2007: | Roll It *(J-Status featuring Shontelle and Rihanna)* |
| 2008: | If I Never See Your Face Again *(Maroon 5 featuring Rihanna)* |
| 2008: | Live Your Life *(T.I. featuring Rihanna)* |
| 2009: | Run This Town *(Jay-Z featuring Rihanna & Kanye West)* |
| 2010: | Love the Way You Lie *(Eminem featuring Rihanna)* |
| 2010: | Who's That Chick *(David Guetta featuring Rihanna)* |
| 2011: | All of the Lights *(Kanye West featuring Rihanna)* |

## ON HER OWN SINGLES

| | |
|---|---|
| 2006: | Break It Off *(featuring Sean Paul)* |
| 2007: | Umbrella *(featuring Jay-Z)* |
| 2007: | Hate that I Love You *(featuring Ne-Yo)* |
| 2009: | Hard *(featuring Jeezy)* |
| 2010: | Rockstar 101 *(featuring Slash)* |
| 2010: | What's My Name *(featuring Drake)* |
| 2010: | Raining Men *(featuring Nicki Minaj)* |

Ok, so music is her first love, but there are plenty more things Rihanna is good at - she's certainly a talented (and very busy) lady!

# OTHER rihanna VENTURES

### Fragrance
Want to smell like RiRi? Her debut perfume, Reb'l Fleur, launched in 2010 under licence with Jay-Z's company, Iconic Fragrances (who else?). The tagline Good Feels so Bad/Bad Feels so Good ties in with hit single S&M, and explores both sides of the singer's personality.

### Charity
Rihanna's Believe Foundation was set up in 2006 to help the lives of terminally ill children

### Ambassador
In 2011, Rihanna was named as a tourism ambassador for her native Barbados. The three-year deal means that the singer has to promote her home island as a great place to go on holiday – pretty easy work, if you ask us!

### Endorsements
Rihanna has modelled for, and her music has helped advertise, lots of brands, including Gucci's Tattoo Heart Collection, Clinique, Nivea, Totes, Nike and CoverGirl.

### Author
Rihanna has launched a coffee table book, Rihanna: The Last Girl on Earth, which is full of never before seen images of the singer on her LGOE tour.

### Actor
Rihanna stars in the film Battleship, a science fiction naval war film, due to be released in 2012.

### Business woman
RiRi has started up her own company, Rihanna Entertainment, so all this hard work can stay under one roof!

we love you... RIHANNA

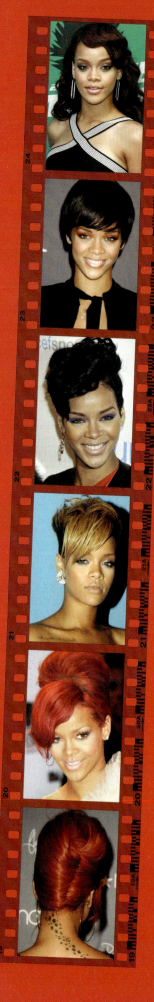
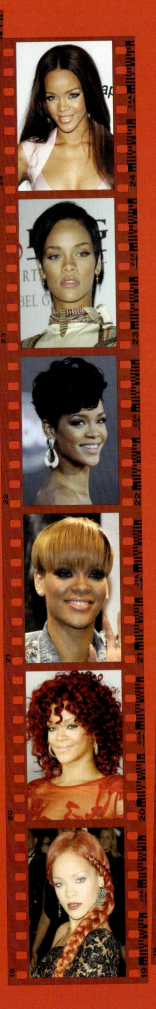

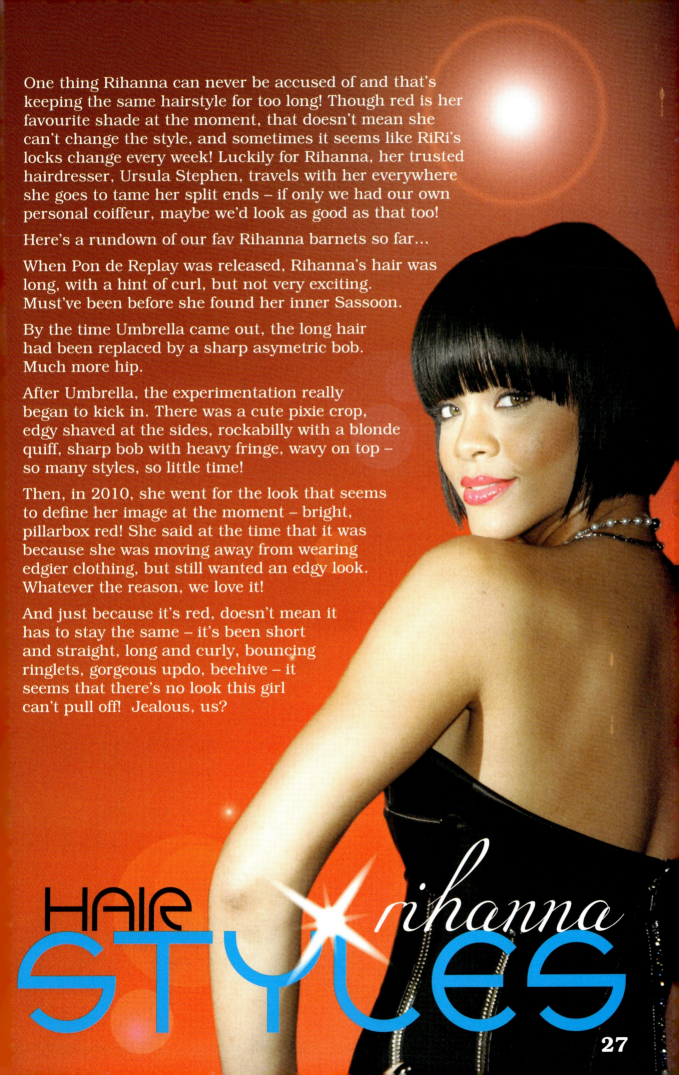

One thing Rihanna can never be accused of and that's keeping the same hairstyle for too long! Though red is her favourite shade at the moment, that doesn't mean she can't change the style, and sometimes it seems like RiRi's locks change every week! Luckily for Rihanna, her trusted hairdresser, Ursula Stephen, travels with her everywhere she goes to tame her split ends – if only we had our own personal coiffeur, maybe we'd look as good as that too!

Here's a rundown of our fav Rihanna barnets so far…

When Pon de Replay was released, Rihanna's hair was long, with a hint of curl, but not very exciting. Must've been before she found her inner Sassoon.

By the time Umbrella came out, the long hair had been replaced by a sharp asymetric bob. Much more hip.

After Umbrella, the experimentation really began to kick in. There was a cute pixie crop, edgy shaved at the sides, rockabilly with a blonde quiff, sharp bob with heavy fringe, wavy on top – so many styles, so little time!

Then, in 2010, she went for the look that seems to define her image at the moment – bright, pillarbox red! She said at the time that it was because she was moving away from wearing edgier clothing, but still wanted an edgy look. Whatever the reason, we love it!

And just because it's red, doesn't mean it has to stay the same – it's been short and straight, long and curly, bouncing ringlets, gorgeous updo, beehive – it seems that there's no look this girl can't pull off! Jealous, us?

# HAIR STYLES rihanna

# CROSSWORD

**ACROSS**

3  RiRi struck a pose on the cover of this magazine in April 2011 (5)
5  This Caribbean style of music is said to influence Rihanna's sound (9)
6  Rihanna was born in this month (8)
7  This singer took part in a raunchy duet with RiRi at the recent Grammy Awards (7)
8  Jay-Z signed our girl to this label (3,3)
9  Last Girl on ........ – global tour Rihanna started in 2009 (5)
12  The beautiful island, Rihanna's home (8)
15  One of the best bits about growing up on a sunny island was visiting this place every day (5)
16  Apple Yonder (anagram). Rihanna's debut single in 2006 (3,2,6)
18  'Never a failure, always a ...............' One of Rihanna's tattoos and her personal motto (6)
19  This kind of 'Love' was sampled on SOS – it was originally a hit in 1981 (7)

**DOWN**

1  RiRi's Superfans – are you one of the ............. (4)
2  Unlucky for some, this is the number of tattoos our girl has – at the moment, anyway! (8)
4  This song went 3 x Platinum in the US in 2007 (8)
10  What breed of dog is Rhianna's pet DJ? (3,6)
11  Janet ............, one of Rihanna's childhood idols (7)
13  This dramatic colour is Rhianna's favourite for her hair right now (3)
14  Reb'l Fleur – a new product by Rihanna that makes her smell sweet (7)
15  Rihanna set up this foundation to help terminally ill children (7)
17  Turn up the volume when you're listening to Rihanna's latest album (4)

**Answers on pages 60.**

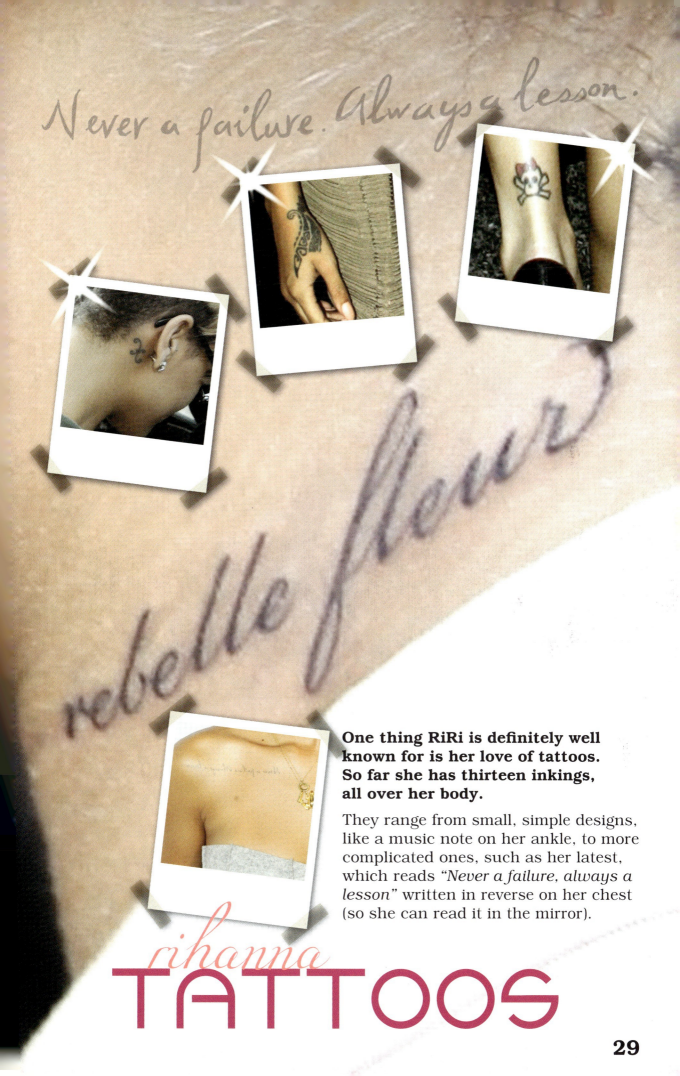

One thing RiRi is definitely well known for is her love of tattoos. So far she has thirteen inkings, all over her body.

They range from small, simple designs, like a music note on her ankle, to more complicated ones, such as her latest, which reads *"Never a failure, always a lesson"* written in reverse on her chest (so she can read it in the mirror).

# rihanna TATTOOS

While her early image may have been a tad too 'girl next door' for some, since then Rihanna has certainly began to channel her inner fashion icon, and loves experimenting with new looks, seeing it as a way to keep things fresh for both herself and her fans. Of course, its great fun dressing up and being styled too – a perk of the job!

For her first two albums, Music of the Sun and A Girl Like Me, RiRi's look was very much bubbly pop starlet – but the release of the video for "Umbrella" saw her experiment a little with textures and colours, but it still wasn't quite her style.

Critics at this time said that Rihanna was trying to become a copy of Beyonce, both musically and in her image, and that led to her taking a different approach to her style.

The video for Shut Up And Drive saw Rihanna take on the role of a sexy mechanic, and all her videos since then have had a definite 'story' with RiRi playing the lead character in each.

Rihanna was voted 17th in Glamour Magazines coveted 50 Most Glamorous Women feature in 2009, and the magazine applauded her for her willingness to take fashion risks (which can go wrong as well as right!).

Her fashion knowledge has now matured, and after a spell wearing edgy, directional clothing, Rihanna has gone back to more 'girly' clothes, but has kept her edge with the pillar box red hair.

She is known for her love of both designer and high street clothing, from H&M and J Crew to Alexander McQueen and Jean Paul Gaultier. She also rocks Nike trainers, GAP underwear and loves a good rummage at vintage stores to perfect her eclectic look.

Though Rihanna has famously stayed very close to her childhood friends, she's picked up a few new ones along the way…

# FAMOUS FRIENDS
*rihanna*

### Katy Perry
The pair holidayed together in Barbados in 2009, and although Rihanna couldn't make Katy's wedding to Russell Brand they still remain close. Katy said, 'My girl organised the best bachelorette party ever and I'll always love her to bits.

### Nicki Minaj
Duetted on "Raining Men", taken from "Loud".

### Beyonce
The rumor-mill went wild with stories of a feud between the two stars, however this is not the case with Rihanna saying of Beyonce, "She is one of the sweetest women I've ever met".

### Eminem
Duetted on 'Love The Way You Lie' and LTWYL Part 2!

### Blake Lively
The Gossip Girl actress and RiRi appeared on top US comedy show, Saturday Night Live together.

### Timbaland
Genius producer has worked on lots of Rihanna's music, and the pair have become good friends.

### Jay-Z
Signed Rihanna to Def Jam, and has remained a close mentor and friend ever since.

### Bob Marley

Growing up in Barbados, Rihanna listened to a lot of reggae, and of course, this meant listening to the late Jamaican legend Bob Marley. In fact, she loves him so much, her new LA mansion has a room dedicated to him – there's a big picture of him on the wall, the room is decorated in green, yellow and red, like the Jamaican flag, and there are lots of books about Bob lying around. She says that as well as his music influencing her, Bob paved the way for other Caribbean artists to succeed on a global scale.

### Madonna

Of course, Rihanna admires Madonna's music, but it's her ability to reinvent herself that really makes her an influence – "I want to be the black Madonna," she said in 2007. RiRi loves to change her look, and has become more daring over the years, and this is something the Material Girl is an expert on. Recently the two have worked together, with Rihanna performing in a fundraiser for Malawi, and helping advertise Vita Coco, a coconut water company Madonna is an investor in.

### Mariah Carey

The legendary songstress and recent mother of twins has been a big influence on Rihanna – in fact, she won a school talent contest singing Mariah's song "Hero". There has been some gossip going round which says the two singers don't get on, but Mariah will always be one of Rihanna's idols.

### Janet Jackson

Rihanna really loves Janet Jackson's energy and vibrancy, and was another artist that she listened to a lot while growing up. Michael's little sister showed Rihanna that even little girls can have the power to command whole arenas, and filled her with confidence for the future.

### Beyonce

It has been reported that Rihanna decided to start a career in the music business after seeing an interview with Beyonce when she was still a part of Destiny's Child. The gossip mongers tried to make out that Beyonce and Rihanna were rivals for Jay-Z's attentions, but the two ladies always seem to be best of friends to us.

*Rihanna has been serious about music from an early age – those horrible critics who at first dismissed her as bubblegum pop didn't know the half of it!*

1: Who did Rihanna holiday with in Barbados 2009?

2: How many weeks did 'Umbrella' stay at the top of the UK charts in 2007?

3: Rihanna might have been dreaming forever if she hadn't met who?

4: Where in Barbados was Rihanna born?

5: Which Destiny's Child song did Rihanna first sing for record producer Evan Rogers?

6: What size of bed does Rihanna sing about in a 2011 single?

7: Which successful female artist does Rihanna admire for the ability to reinvent herself?

8: Which well-respected fashion magazine did Rihanna become a covergirl for in April 2011?

9: What is Reb'L Fleur?

10: Which 2009 concert put on by Jay-Z did Rihanna perform at?

Answers on page 61.

# QUIZ QUESTIONS
*rihanna*

# MATCH UP *rihanna*

Can you match the legs to the right outfit?

Answers on page 60.

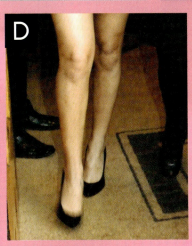

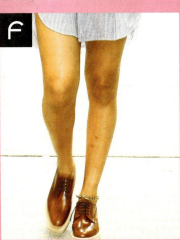

Though she's just in her early twenties, Rihanna has already won heaps of awards all over the world. Here's a list of the most special – there's just not enough room to list them all! In total, to date, she has been nominated a massive 216 times and out of that won 97 times. And the awards just keep coming…

**American Music Awards**
Favourite Female Artist – Soul/R&B
Won 2007, 2008, 2010

Favourite Female Artist – Pop/Rock
Won 2008

**Barbados Music Awards**
Since 2006, Rihanna has been nominated for these awards 43 times, and won 33 of these

**Billboard Music Awards**
These awards are based on sales in the US. Nominated 33 times, won 18 awards

**Brit Awards**
Won Best International Female Artist in 2011

**Grammy**
Rihanna has won four prestigious Grammy Awards for Umbrella, Run This Town and Only Girl (In The World)

**MTV Europe Music Awards**
Two wins

**MTV Video Music Awards**
Two wins (both for Umbrella)

**People's Choice Awards**
Five awards won

**Teen Choice**
Five awards won

1. Rihanna went to Combermere High School?
   *FACT or FICTION*

2. Rihanna is signed to Red Jam Records?
   *FACT or FICTION*

3. Rihanna means Sweet Basil?
   *FACT or FICTION*

4. Rihanna has a musical note tattoo on her ear?
   *FACT or FICTION*

5. Rihanna's single Unfaithful was written by Ne-Yo?
   *FACT or FICTION*

6. Rihanna doesn't listen to music?
   *FACT or FICTION*

7. Rihanna had a cameo role in Bring It On: All Or Nothing in 2006?
   *FACT or FICTION*

8. Rihanna's single Umbrella was about the British weather?
   *FACT or FICTION*

9. Rihanna's drill sergeant at cadets when she was younger was fellow singer Shontelle?
   *FACT or FICTION*

10. Rihanna doesn't like the beach?
    *FACT or FICTION*

11. Rihanna's single Rehab was co-written by Justin Timberlake?
    *FACT or FICTION*

12. Rihanna Navy is about her love for dark blue?
    *FACT or FICTION*

13. Rihanna was born to be a star?
    *FACT or FICTION*

JUST FOR FUN
FACT OR FICTION?
rihanna

Rihanna's superfans, the Rihanna Navy are the official street team for Rihanna, supporting her 24/7! Formed via online chatrooms and their Facebook page, the Navy (a reference to RiRi's background in Army Cadets) have become a strong voice, and one, it seems, that Rihanna actually listens to!

**In their own words:**
RihannaNavy is not just a fanbase, not just a movement but a group of people who have the same point of interest (read: Rihanna) and became friends.

With over 32 million fans on Facebook, Rihanna loves the way she can get an instant reaction to any of her work:

"It is important for me professionally because I get to really get the first feedback you know, right away. I don't have to think about it, I don't have to guess."

And the Navy are to thank for that the Britney remix of S&M – using Twitter to ask Ri and Brit to work together, and hey presto, they did it!

They're called Rihanna Navy as a reference a line in her song Gangster 4Life (G4L), which says "We're an army. Better yet a *navy*. Better yet crazy!"

They know almost everything about the singer, watching her tweets very carefully to see who she follows, and more importantly, doesn't follow.

It was rumoured that Rihanna was even going to record a song named after them, but nothing has been confirmed, yet!

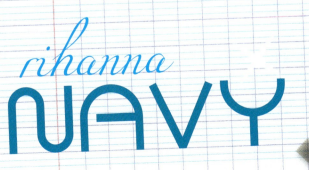

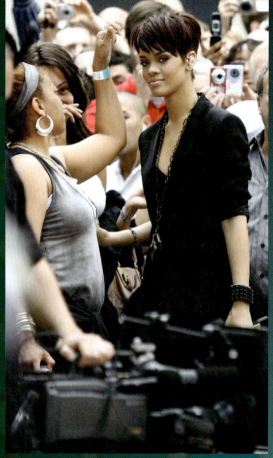

**Can you spot ten differences in these two pictures of Ri?**

**Answers on page 61.**

# SPOT THE
# DIFFERENCE

**Rihanna didn't have what you might call a privileged upbringing, but despite that, even at an early age, she knew that she wanted to help others:**

"When I was young and I would watch television and I would see all the children suffering, I always said: when I grow up, I want to help."

Her success as an artist has allowed her to help many different people in many different ways. Rihanna launched her Believe Foundation in 2006 to help terminally ill children.

The Foundation is committed to helping change the lives of young people by providing educational, financial, social and medical support when and wherever it is needed.

As part of her work to support Believe, Rihanna took part in a series of concerts in 2008 to help promote and raise money for the Foundation.

Rihanna has performed a number of concerts to raise funds for both charities and the Foundation and is a 2008 Cartier Love Charity Bracelet Ambassador. She performed at Madonna's Raising Malawi fundraiser in 2008.

– the t-shirts read "Believe" and "Stop and Think", and she even stopped to sign some for a few lucky shoppers!

In August 2008, Rihanna and other artists, including Beyonce recorded the charity single, "Just Stand Up!", the theme song to the anti-cancer campaign Stand Up to Cancer.

Rihanna was also selected as the spokesmodel for Gucci's first United Nations Children's Fund ad campaign, and photographed in a series of special edition print ads.

Rihanna performed on January 20, 2009, at the Recording Industry Association of America's Presidential Inauguration Charity Ball to raise money for the world's largest anti-hunger organization.

In September 2009, Rihanna performed at Jay-Z's "Answer the Call" concert, which paid tribute to the police officers and firefighters who died on the September 11 attacks. Our girl has also been a part of many benefit concerts to help raise money for various illnesses, such as cancer for Hope Rocks. In January 2010 she performed live with Bono on stage at the 'Hope For Haiti Now: A Global Benefit For Earthquake Relief' in London.

# rihanna's CHARITIES

In her role of honorary cultural ambassador for Barbados, Rihanna became involved with DKMS, an international donor network based in Germany, to try to find a donor for a mother in New York suffering from leukemia.

Rihanna also supports AIDS charities and designed a t-shirt for H&M during the Fashion Against AIDS campaign

On being discovered by song writers and producers Evan Rogers and Carl Sturken: *"If I hadn't met Evan and Carl I might have just been dreaming forever."* On the kind of music she likes to make: *"When I purchase an album, I like an album where I don't have to skip any song, that's the kind of album I tried to make. There's something on there for everyone, up tempos, mid tempos, some ballads, some old-school reggae."* On Beyonce: *"Beyonce just put the level of female entertainment all the way up there. She does acting, she has a beautiful voice and that's really the person I look up to... that type of entertainer."* On success: *"Success for me isn't a destination it's a journey. Everybody's working to get to the top but where is the top? It's all about working harder and getting better and moving up and up."* On why she decided to dye her hair red: *"With my hair I was ready for something new, something loud, something expressive and something fun. I'd had blonde hair and it was so boring for me. Black is still my favourite colour, but this time I wanted something edgier because I don't like the edgy clothes any more. I guess I had to take the edge to somewhere else – my hair!"* On how she's liking acting (in new film Battleship): *"It's really good, really good. I'm really enjoying it actually."* On relaxing: *"I love it when I get those days where I don't have a specific time to get out of bed. On those days where I don't have anything to do I just lay in bed and watch TV all day. It is heaven! A day of Family Guy and comedy. Great!"* On starting a family: *"I'm really scared of the actual childbirth situation but I do want to be a mom one day. Even if I have to adopt, I want to be a mom."* On what she likes in a man: *"Definitely a guy with a sense of humour because I love to laugh. Someone who doesn't take themselves too seriously, who likes to have fun – it should all be fun. Being in a relationship should be something that is exciting and makes you happy, so if the guy makes me happy, then he gets a chance."* On meeting Jay-Z for the first time: *"When I met with Jay-Z, I was so scared. I was shaking. But the minute I went into his office, he was so warm and welcoming that he really made me feel at home."* On singing: *"I would sing in the mirror, holding a brush to my mouth like it was a microphone. The neighbours would always be complaining about how loud I was singing."* On Reb'l Fleur: *"This fragrance is about my passion for individuality being expressive and empowering – but also emotional and intriguing."* On making music videos: *"S&M is my favourite video that I've ever, ever, ever done. I can't wait to keep making more incredible videos."* On the Union Jack: *"I think the British flag is the most fashionable flag there is!"*

# rihanna's SAY WHAT?

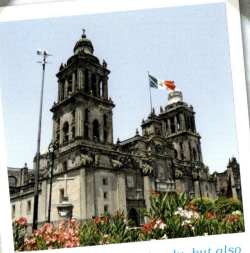
**Place:** Barbados, obviously, but also Mexico and the South of France

**Snack:** Lemon and Garlic Olives

**Gadget:** iPad

**Performers:** Jay-Z and Paramore

# rihanna's FAVOURITE THINGS

**Jeans:** *H&M and J Brand*

**Designer:** *Jean Paul Gaultier*

**Dessert:** *Red Velvet Cake*

**Films:** *Pineapple Express, The Hangover, Superbad, Borat*

**Bag:** *She has plenty but is seen out with her Prada Denim Bag lots*

**Perfume:** *Reb'l Fleur (of course!)*

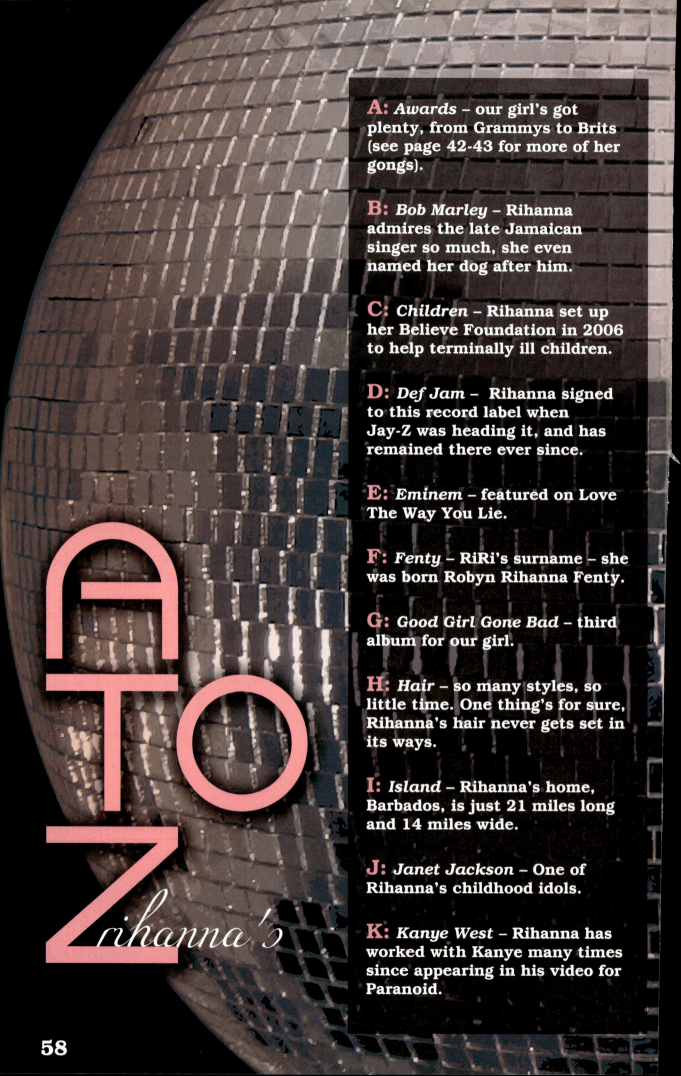

# A TO Z
## rihanna's

**A:** *Awards* – our girl's got plenty, from Grammys to Brits (see page 42-43 for more of her gongs).

**B:** *Bob Marley* – Rihanna admires the late Jamaican singer so much, she even named her dog after him.

**C:** *Children* – Rihanna set up her Believe Foundation in 2006 to help terminally ill children.

**D:** *Def Jam* – Rihanna signed to this record label when Jay-Z was heading it, and has remained there ever since.

**E:** *Eminem* – featured on Love The Way You Lie.

**F:** *Fenty* – RiRi's surname – she was born Robyn Rihanna Fenty.

**G:** *Good Girl Gone Bad* – third album for our girl.

**H:** *Hair* – so many styles, so little time. One thing's for sure, Rihanna's hair never gets set in its ways.

**I:** *Island* – Rihanna's home, Barbados, is just 21 miles long and 14 miles wide.

**J:** *Janet Jackson* – One of Rihanna's childhood idols.

**K:** *Kanye West* – Rihanna has worked with Kanye many times since appearing in his video for Paranoid.

**L:** *Loud* – Rihanna's fifth album sold 207,000 copies in its first week of release.

**M:** *Mariah Carey* – another idol. Rihanna won a talent contest at school singing Carey's Hero.

**N:** *Navy* – Rihanna's super fans call themselves the Navy and are very well respected - it's said that her duet with Britney at the 2011 Grammys was down to them.

**O:** *Oh na na na na, c'mon* – this could be the catchiest hook ever!

**P:** *Pon de Replay* – Rihanna's debut single was a huge hit across the globe.

**Q:** *Quotes* – Rihanna likes to speak her mind, and is not afraid to air her feelings on Twitter or through her website.

**R:** *Reb'l Fleur* – the debut fragrance from the singer was launched in 2011.

**S:** *Saint Michael* – The town in Barbados where Rihanna was born and grew up.

**T:** *Tattoos* – at the last count RiRi has 13, including a music note on her ankle and a trail of stars down the back of her neck.

**U:** *Umbrella* – Was number 1 for 10 weeks in the UK back in the summer of 2007 and was blamed for the bad weather.

**V:** *Vogue* – fashion-loving Rihanna was the covergirl for US Vogue in April 2011.

**W:** *What's My Name?* – Hit number 1 on the UK in January 2011, and meant Rihanna became the first female solo artist to have five number 1 singles in the UK in consecutive years.

**X:** *X-Rated* – 2011 hit single S&M was thought to be so naughty it had to have a 'clean' option for some radio stations...

**Y:** *Yes, sir* – RiRi probably had to say this during her time in the Bajan Army Cadets.

**Z:** *Jay-Z* – the music mogul first signed Rihanna to Def Jam and featured her in his hit single Run This Town.

# QUIZ ANSWERS

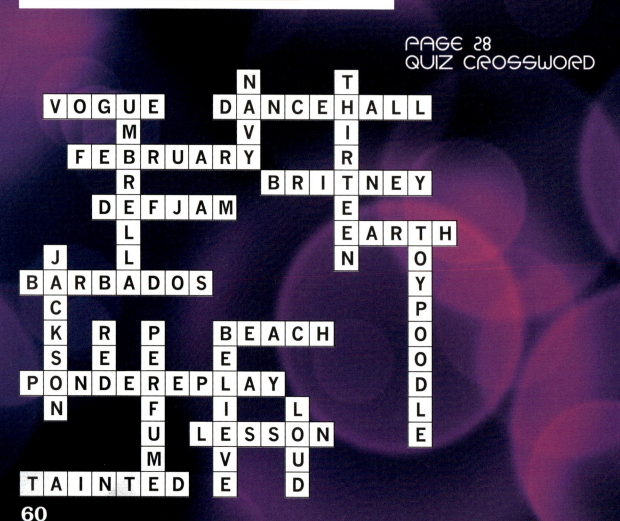

PAGE 12
WORDSEARCH

PAGE 28
QUIZ CROSSWORD

## PAGE 44
## FACT OR FICTION?

1. FACT
2. FICTION
3. FACT
4. FICTION
5. FACT
6. FICTION
7. FACT
8. FICTION
9. FACT
10. FICTION
11. FACT
12. FICTION
13. FACT

## PAGE 40
## MATCH UP

1. d
2. e
3. f
4. a
5. b
6. c

## PAGE 39
## QUIZ TIME ANSWERS

1. Katy Perry
2. 10 weeks
3. Evan and Carl
4. Saint Michael
5. Emotion
6. California King Bed
7. Madonna
8. US Vogue
9. Rihanna's new perfume, released in 2011
10. Answer The Call

## PAGE 48
## SPOT THE DIFFERENCE

## PAGE 44
## FACT OR FICTION?

1. FACT
2. FICTION
3. FACT
4. FICTION
5. FACT
6. FICTION
7. FACT
8. FICTION
9. FACT
10. FICTION
11. FACT
12. FICTION
13. FACT

## PAGE 40
## MATCH UP

1. d
2. e
3. f
4. a
5. b
6. c

## PAGE 39
## QUIZ TIME ANSWERS

1. Katy Perry
2. 10 weeks
3. Evan and Carl
4. Saint Michael
5. Emotion
6. California King Bed
7. Madonna
8. US Vogue
9. Rihanna's new perfume, released in 2011
10. Answer The Call

## PAGE 48
## SPOT THE DIFFERENCE